WELLS

IN OLD PHOTOGRAPHS

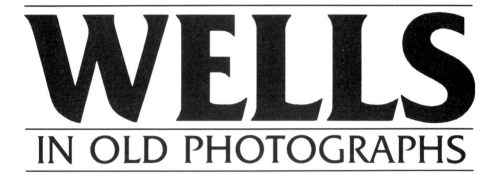

WELLS

IN OLD PHOTOGRAPHS

COLLECTED BY

CHRIS HOWELL

ALAN SUTTON
1989

Alan Sutton Publishing
Gloucester

First Published 1989

British Library Cataloguing in Publication Data

Wells in old photographs.
I. Howell, Chris
942.3'83

ISBN 0-86299-688-0

Typesetting and origination by
Alan Sutton Publishing
Printed in Great Britain by
Dotesios Printers Limited

CONTENTS

FOREWORD

In a place like Wells it is impossible to ignore history. It is all around us: the majestic Cathedral, the beautiful Palace and grounds, the historic Market Place – all these monuments and more speak of the past. But we often forget that such historic places were peopled by men and women just like you and me.

One of the reasons why I am very happy to write a Foreword to Chris Howell's book is that he makes the past live. He weaves together pictures of real people and familiar places with commentaries from those who lived at the time when the photographs were taken. What comes across is the authentic voice of ordinary people who interpret for us the world they inhabited. Sometimes this is done humorously, sometimes very prosaically – but always freshly and humanly.

I hope Chris Howell's book sells very well. It deserves to, because only by treasuring the past can we truly live as fulfilled human beings.

George Carey
Bishop of Bath and Wells

INTRODUCTION

I like Wells. Although I have never lived there I do have close connections with the city and some of my earliest memories are to do with the place. My father, who was in the Far East for much of the last war, returned on compassionate grounds to be with his parents who were both very elderly with only a short time to live. As their home was only a few miles from Wells he was posted, as Adjutant, to the German prisoner-of-war camp that was then at Stoberry Park. I was four or five at the time and sometimes visited him with my mother and, when I did, I was allowed to play with the German soldiers in their compound. They were always extraordinarily kind to me and I remember that I was greatly excited and proud whenever I went there.

It is now 45 years since the war and the camp has gone. There is now a small housing estate and a pair of schools where it once stood. By happy coincidence my wife is the head teacher of one of these schools, caring for the four and five-year-olds who now play in the grounds as I once did.

This year Wells has celebrated the 400th anniversary of the charters granted by Queen Elizabeth I which allowed its people to manage their own affairs. While much of the fabric of the city remains the same as it did in 1589 (though compare the pictures on pages 26 and 27!) there are other things in and around Wells that have changed imperceptibly. One evening during my research I came across a news item from 1912 that reported the then remarkable sighting of no fewer than 15 seagulls over Wells and yet, on my way home over the Mendips, I spotted three or four hundred of them following a plough – a common enough sight these days.

Wells is a beautiful little city with great charm; an intriguing history and a delightfully modest way with visitors. But what has given me the greatest pleasure during the past months has been meeting and talking to the people who live there and love the place. I have yet to meet anyone who does not feel at ease there. I hope that by using their pictures and their memories I have served them and their city well.

Chris Howell
Chilcompton
August 1989

The Cathedral

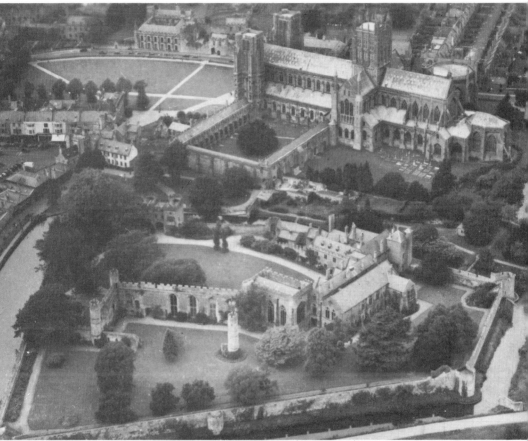

'... THE CATHEDRAL, the Palace, the Cloister, the Chapter House, the Vicars' Close, the Deanery, the detached houses of the Canons ... which altogether make up this unique and lovely city, still almost perfect, still almost as it was in the Middle Ages. The view is unique; it cannot, in its completeness, be matched in Europe, and, as it were at a glance, it gives you the history of Wells from its beginning in the eighth century till our own day.' (Edward Hutton in 1919.)

'GRANDFATHER WAS CALLED VINNELL — French, so called — Fred Vinnell, and in 1907 he made a little stone man and set it up in the back tower of the cathedral. Every day after school I'd get a jug of tea from Mother and scurry up the tower like mad so's he'd have it before it went cold.' (IH.)

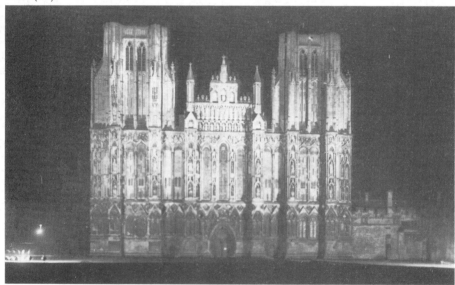

'RATHER SPLENDID, illuminated like that, isn't it. It was done during the carnival week of 1935 or 6. Nothing like when I first saw it in 1911. Then it was dirty and rather rough-looking and covered in scaffolding set in heavy barrels and held together with twisted wire.' (SF.)

'THE OLD SPRINGS OF WELLS are in here, in the Palace gardens. Really they're the wells from which the place gets its name – three big ones and lots of little ones. When they built the tower that you see here they found that it put an immense strain on the foundations of the building – the cracks can still be seen in places to this day – and that's when they had to build the great inverted strainer arches inside to take the weight.' (AR.)

'WHAT A MAGNIFICENT SIGHT THAT NAVE IS. When I first saw it in 1911 there were none of those chairs there – it looked like it must have done in the olden days. See the 'OXO' sign? Made by the great arches when they were built in the 1300s because of the trouble the tower created on the south side. The Owl Arches the locals used to call them. See the great eyes?' (SF.)

'UP ABOVE THE STRAINER ARCH opposite is where they put the statues of the Lord, Mary and John – life-size figures when they're down at ground level. Outside, on the West Front, there were 300 statues once – put there by Bishop Jocelyn, a local boy – but some have fallen off now. Once upon a time they were all painted in bright colours, and if you can get up there you can still find traces of red and blue and gold and silver and green on their backs today.' (FG.)

'THESE ARE THE LOVELY CLOISTERS on the east side and that door at the end leads into the South Transept. This is where I used to race along with Grandfather's tea to keep it warm.' (IH.)

'NOW, THESE GREAT STEPS lead up to the Chapter House and you can go through that door, there, to get you over Chain Gate to Vicars' Close. Another thing Grandfather did was to turn all these huge steps over 'cause they were getting so worn. I used to sit and watch him while he did it.' (IH.)

'JACK BLANDIVER, the quarter-jack; Lazy Jack, who kicks the bells with his heels to set the two clocks striking. Been doing that for 500 years. He's reputed to stand for nobody – not even the Queen. He's always been there.' (AR.)

'THIS IS THE FINE OLD CLOCK next to Jack Blandiver. Twenty-four hours, with the minutes marked off by the star. See the knights at the top? Every hour four of them chase each other round and round – jousting till one of them gets knocked off.' (JS.)

'THIS IS THE CLOCK on the northern side of the Cathedral and while the knights inside are haring round with their jousting exercise these two are outside belting the bells with their battle-axes.' (JS.)

'A SUPERB VIEW! Taken from Tor Hill before the Great War when we used to go there for our Sunday School outings. Running races and things and winning boxes of paints and suchlike. Oh, bless your heart, yes.' (IH.)

SECTION TWO

The Medieval City

'THE MOAT AROUND THE BISHOP'S PALACE is fed by the wells in the Palace garden in that earlier picture [page 11] but the only time it was put to its intended use was when there was some rioting at the Bishop's Palace in Bristol in 1830 something, and because of that they pulled up the drawbridge here in Wells, just in case. But there was no need – nothing happened.' (FG.)

'THE GATEHOUSE AND DRAWBRIDGE to the Bishop's Palace were built in the 1300s by Bishop Ralph when there was a bit of trouble between the local people and the Church. Can't pull the drawbridge up today – even if there is trouble – 'cause 'tis made of concrete.' (FG.)

'AMONG THE BEAUTIFUL MEDIEVAL HOUSES of the West of England the Bishop's Palace at Wells takes a very prominent place. Not to see it . . . is not to see Wells . . . it has a special beauty of its own which is hardly surpassed anywhere in England.' (*Country Life* – 1913.)

'MY FRIEND LIVED THERE in the Bishop's Palace and I've fed the swans from that window heaps of times. The swans would ring the bell on the wall at four o'clock for their food and all the birds would turn up to be fed – ducks an' all. 'Tisn't done quite so much these days – depends who lives there to train them.' (IH.)

'THIS IS BISHOP BECKINGTON'S WELL-HOUSE in the gardens of the Bishop's Palace. He had this built to pump the water from his grounds to the conduit in the Market Place [see page 148]. Clever chap, he was, and no mistake.' (TT.)

'SEE THE SHOPS IN THE MARKET PLACE, through the archway there? This is the Bishop's Eye, of course, built by Bishop Beckington, and hidden under all that ivy on the left is one of his rebuses [see page 24].' (JS.)

PENNILESS PORCH (on the left) and the Bishop's Eye, seen in the 1930s. 'The Porch used to be called the Beggar's Eye. Two or three blind men used to stand in there all day long with their little enamel cups – right back in the corner. Then you'd see someone come to empty them for them every-so-often.' (IH.)

'PENNILESS PORCH, connecting the Cathedral Green with the Market Place, was also built by Bishop Beckington and up on the right there you can see his rebus – that's like his name in a picture. It's made up of a flaming tar barrel on a pole, or a signal (a beck) in a barrel (a tun). Beck-in-tun, get it?' (F.G.)

'CAW, THIS IS AN OLD ONE. Looks like they're stone masons doing up the Theological College a bit. On Cathedral Green. Nowadays its the music part of the Cathedral School but before that they trained vicars there for 100 years or more.' (TT.)

'CHAIN GATE, here, was built by Bishop Beckington so's the 44 vicars could walk through the passageway from Vicars' Close and get into the Cathedral without mixing with the *hoi polloi* in Wells. Some of them used to get up to naughty things before, see.' (FG.)

'THIS PICTURE IS OLDER THAN THE OTHER ONE 'cause that looks like a shop on the right and that must've gone long ago. See those two ghosts by the horse? And see how those pinnacles are crumbling and worn away? They're not like that in the other picture 'cause Grandfather repaired them.' (IH.)

'VICARS' CLOSE is said to be the oldest inhabited street in Europe, dating from the middle of the fourteenth century. It was founded by Bishop Ralph for the vicars. Now, when I say 'vicars' I don't mean priests, I mean choirmen. A vicar is a choirman, and a vicar priest is a deacon.' (AR.)

'VICARS' CLOSE AGAIN. At one time all that middle part was grassed over like you'd find at the old universities. Down at the end you can see the door leading to the kitchen and dining room where all the vicars ate together. And beyond that is Chain Gate.' (FG.)

'I LOVE VICARS' CLOSE. Often go up there. There's a little chapel at the top. Been in there? There's nothing to stop you. Go in quietly in case there's someone in there trying to mesmerise his thoughts.' (IH.)

'THE OLD DEANERY, on Cathedral Green – lovely building. Was the Dean's residence for well over 700 years but no Dean has lived there now since Dr Woodford's time. Used as the Diocesan offices nowadays.' (FG.)

'LLEWELLYN'S ALMSHOUSES, down off Priest Row, were given by a chap called Llewellyn who was Mayor of Wells at the beginning of the seventeenth century. They're for ladies only. Pretty little houses.' (FG.)

'BUBWITH'S ALMSHOUSES. I used to come here delivering eggs over 80 years ago – ha'penny for small ones, penny for big. I loved to talk to the dear old souls in their special uniforms – hats and bonnets and capes and things. Always wanted to live here and now I do!' (IH.)

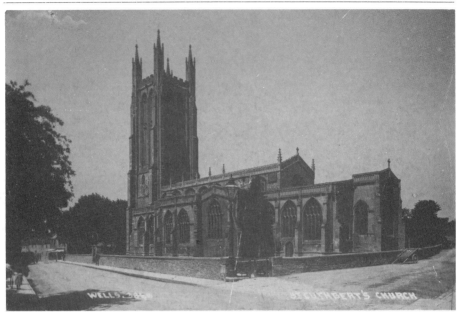

'FANCY HAVING ST CUTHBERT'S CHURCH IN WELLS as well as the Cathedral! Such a beautiful church. More than once I've found visitors there thinking they were at the Cathedral – and you can hardly blame them.' (IH.)

'DID YOU KNOW that St Cuthbert's had men and horses billeted in it during the Monmouth Rebellion? And that it used to be the town's gunpowder store? That's Bubwith's Almshouses on the left and down the front is where they built the Boys' Blue School. This must be very old.' (TT.)

Wells and Royalty

'OLD JOHN HOLLOWAY – the Alderman – used to deck out his shop in the Market Place for the slightest excuse, and Victoria's Jubilee in 1887 was as good as any. He used to have crimson drapes on the walls, pictures of the royal family in the windows, red white and blue flags and bunting and anything else that showed how patriotic he was. Quite a sight it was too.' (TT.)

'I RECKON THAT THIS ARCHWAY was built by the people at The Globe — they always did a lot for the carnivals and fairs and things. This one was for Edward VII's Coronation in 1902 — all done with greenery and stuff. I fancy that a Mr Perrin built another one here in Priest Row for Victoria's Jubilee in 1887.' (IH.)

'THIS IS ANTIQUE, ISN'T IT! The Town Crier should be in front of this little lot somewhere 'cause it's the Mayor and Corporation. See the little glass candleholders up above the word CLUB? They're in the shape of an R – part of ER, 'cause this was taken at the time of the Coronation in 1902.' (FG.)

'SEE HOW IT SAYS "GOD SAVE..." up on the Town Hall? Everyone was there for Edward's Coronation do in 1902. And see, right at the back, the fire brigade have come out of the fire station to be in the picture? And see how the post office building is still all pillars on the left – wasn't filled in for about another year after this was taken. Interesting.' (TT.)

'I WAS THERE when the Prince and Princess of Wales came. It was because of the Millenary – when the Bishopric was 1,000 years old. They were on their way up to the Cathedral for a special service when this was taken and had just stopped for a moment to chat to the Mayor and his committee.' 22 June 1909. (IH.)

'AFTER THE SERVICE was over they were taken over the Green and through Brown's Gate for a meal at the Bishop's place. Those soldiers on horseback behind them are in the North Somerset Yeomanry. Knew some of them.' (IH.)

'FOR THAT ROYAL VISIT my school was stuck right back by the post office and I couldn't see anything. Now I'd gone there intending to see, and if I make my mind up to do something then I do it, so I ran out of line – past the kids from the Blue School in their straw hats – and came out by Mr Phillips's shop. Bang opposite the Prince and Princess. Nobody missed me. If they had done I wouldn't have cared.' (IH.)

'AFTER ALL THE SERVICES and ceremonies and things in Wells the Prince and Princess had to go on to Glastonbury for the Restoration of the Abbey there. Got a good turnout here in Wells didn't they!' (TT.)

'WHEN THE CATHEDRAL SERVICE for Edward VII was over, there was – as usual – a procession and this is where the thing was forming up. That's all the staff of the Great Western Railway in Wells lining up outside the Anchor Inn. See Mr Randall, the station master, at the front? Every one of them had brand new uniforms on that day.' (TT.)

'WE HAD A BIG DO for the Coronation in 1911. A very special do on that particular day. There were all sorts of happenings – special teas, sports matches and so on. Kiddies were brought in from the villages in farm wagons lined with straw on the floors. Such fun. A marvellous event and no mistake.' (SF.)

'FOR THAT CORONATION they set up all these trestle tables, and improvisionalised toilets, in the park for we kiddies to have a feast of sticky buns and things. Happy days. See the men at the back there, behind the screen? That was where the local quoits team used to meet. That was their hut with the white roof. Looks like business as usual for them, celebration or no celebration.' (TT.)

GEORGE V was crowned two years to the day after he came to Wells for the Millenary festival and, once again, Wells celebrated the event with a procession. Here the Fire Brigade waits to lead the way through the city.

BEHIND THE FIRE BRIGADE came the Mayor and Corporation – but not before this lady had had her photograph taken.

SECTION FOUR

The Carnivals

CITY DIGNITARIES, carnival committee members, collectors and clowns, as well as a dancing bear (a rather threadbare bear) and a bewildered dog (the forerunner of HMV in Wells?) pose for this study in front of the Bishop's Barn in 1905. The stickers on the collecting boxes read 'contributions solicited'.

THERE WERE 26 FLOATS in the carnival held in 1902 to celebrate Coronation Day. This one, which was called Veterans of the South African War, was led by Corporal Brown of the Royal Engineers.

ANOTHER OF THE ENTRIES for the 1902 Coronation Carnival. This was the crank axle milk cart belonging to Mr E. White of East Wells. The delivery men are Charlie Inge and Ted Hunt.

'WHAT ON EARTH ARE THOSE RED CROSS MEN IN? That's a farm waggon – for hauling hay! I used to do my Red Cross on the chicken farm – setting broken legs for chickens? I'd cut a biggish cabbage stump in half and scoop it out and then bind it on to the leg of the fowl. Right as rain, it'd be.' (IH.)

WELLS FIRE BRIGADE, led by Captain Halliday, turned out for the 1902 Coronation Carnival procession. The brigade was founded in 1874. 'I don't know what this contraption is that they've dolled up, but I remember when they had a little box affair that three or four men would grab hold of and then go belting off to fight fires with.' (IH.)

THESE ENTRANTS in the December Carnival of 1906 called themselves the 'West Indians'. 'Whadda they mean – West Indians? They're meant to be Red Indians, aren't they? Vicious lookin' lot. They came to our shop for the turkey feathers and things for their head-dresses.' (IH.)

AS THE DATE IS WEDNESDAY, 7 November, this is probably the Carnival of 1890 – the poster proclaims that it would be the 'grandest pageant in England'. The gents present for the picture were Messrs Ashton, Silcox, Turner and Hains.

WELLS STEAM LAUNDRY ('Best work – Reasonable charges – Prompt returns') won one of the first prizes given at the 1908 Carnival. Representing them here are Mrs Rowland and her daughter, Mrs Lapham, Mr Cook and Mr and Mrs Horner and Mr Brooks (the cleaner?).

'A MAN CALLED SAY, from Croscombe, used to build these bonfires for the carnivals – I wouldn't know him if I saw him but that's Sidney Tom sitting there with the moustache and the posh coat on. Sidney Thomas Richards, builder and decorator. And I reckon that's Mr Boswell in the white trousers – got pushed to Glastonbury and back in a wheelbarrow once, for a bet of a couple of pints of beer. Just for a lark. Nice people.' (IH.) 1905.

'THIS IS ANOTHER ONE OF THE CARNIVAL BONFIRES and it must have been the year after 'cause I was seven. Can you see the man at the top is leaning against a barrel? That was full of tar and when the fire was lit it all poured down the sides and made a terrific blaze. We kids all had to run away. I wasn't s'posed to be there – but I was!' (IH.)

'WELL. BILL BAILEY MAY WELL HAVE BEEN DEAD, but these aren't his sisters! This is a couple of the lads dressed up to collect for one of the carnivals around 1907 or 8.' (TT.)

City Events

'I WENT TO WATCH whenever the Judge came to Wells for the Assizes. He'd always come to the Cathedral for the service and look so nice in his robes and beautiful colours with his funkies along with him. That's Tom Bailey on the right with the trumpet – the Town Hall Keeper – used to be in the Town Band.' (IH.)

THE HON. G.H. JOLLIFFE (with his hand raised above the letter *E*) addressing the crowds during his 1885 election campaign. Jolliffe – who later became Lord Hylton – was returned as the Conservative member for Wells; beating his Liberal opponent by 4,696 votes to 3,286. Feelings ran very high during this election, which probably accounts for the considerable number of policemen present on this occasion – there are at least 22 in the picture, with five of them stationed in the doorway of the Constitutional Club.

'I'M PRETTY CERTAIN that this was some sort of recruiting meeting during the Boer War. See the soldiers in the front? And they're nearly all young men close to the platform. I remember seeing a number of them when they came back after that war – blue suits they wore, with red stripes down the sides of their trousers.' (IH.)

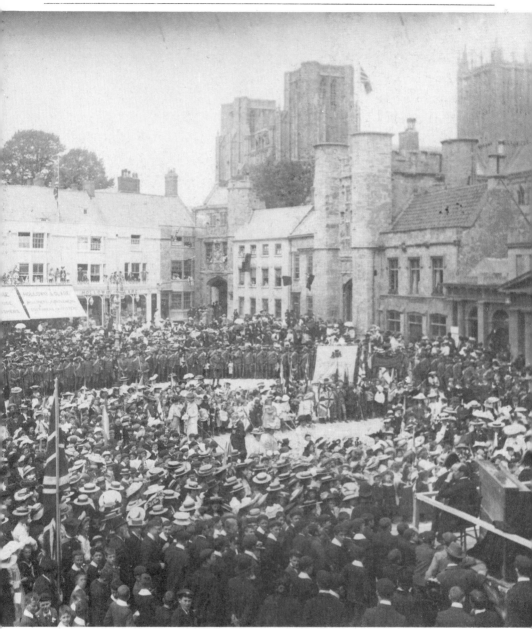

EMPIRE DAY fell on 24 May in 1905 and, as usual, the people of Wells turned out in great numbers. There were well over 1,000 schoolchildren present, with those from Wookey being carried into Wells in horse-drawn brakes. Young Harry Brown can be seen holding the Union Jack and the lady at the piano is Miss Woods from the Blue School. Two squadrons of the Gloucestershire Yeomanry provided the military presence.

EMPIRE DAY, 1907. One of the young ladies, standing outside Mr Dyer's tailoring establishment on the left, was Polly, who used this postcard to write to her friend Ettie in Bath. The message was brief and to the point: 'Here, you took my combinations back with you. Send me another pair'.

'EMPIRE DAY in 1909. That must have been the fourth of those things that I went on – at the back in this one – by the Central School banner. We used to carry the thing in all the parades and woe betide you if you let go one of the cords!' (IH.)

'CAPTAIN SANDYS doing some last minute vote-catching in 1910. He was in the Boer War and then got himself wounded in the Great War with the Life Guards. From the look of his driver's coat it must have been a bit nippy that day. And just look at his wife's hat box on the car roof. Blimey!' (TT.)

EXTRA POLICE were drafted into Wells for an expected large public turnout for the result of the 1910 poll. In the event a crowd of 3,000 gathered outside the Town Hall to learn that Captain Sandys – a Conservative – had beaten his Liberal opponent, a Mr Silcock, by 6,167 votes to 4,871.

A RALLY of early motor cars and tricycles in the Market Place in the autumn of 1901. Among the cars are a Daimler, two De Dion Boutons and two MMCs, as well as two others that defy identification.

'I REMEMBER WHEN THESE PEOPLE CAME HERE IN 1910 – the Northumberland Fusiliers – in the middle of the night when the railways were quiet. They woke me up at three in the morning singing as they marched through the High Street on the way to their camp at Masbury. I ask you! Singing at three in the morning!' (IH.)

'THAT'S ME ON THE LEFT. This is 1913 on the morning when Mr Corbett Wilson landed his plane out on the Park. You can just see the wing at the back there. 'Course we all nipped out to see the thing – it was a wonderful machine.' (GC.)

MR B.C. HUCKS brought his Bleriot monoplane to Wells at the invitation of the Amateur Athletic Union in July 1913. During his demonstration he flew between the towers of the Cathedral. 'There was a fuss about that – I reckon they were afraid he'd knock the things down! He came back on another occasion – when we had a sports meeting. I'd never beaten Hector Bailey over 100 yards before but that day I did and I got to go up in the plane for a prize. Someone else could go too, so Mother paid for Elsie – 'cause she wanted me to pair up with her. Then I paid for Nellie to go up. I married Nellie.' (GC.)

'THAT'S THE CATHEDRAL'S BIRTHDAY DO AGAIN [see pages 37–39] in 1909. That afternoon lots of us went down to Glastonbury on the train for their activities – t'was only a few pence there and back – and then came back here for parties and concerts and fireworks in the evening.' (TT.)

DR ST JOHN BASIL WYNNE WILSON was enthroned as the Bishop of Bath and Wells on 15 November 1921. 'I fancy he was related to the Wills tobacco people of Bristol. He provided a cottage for the head gardener – Sam Cains had it at one time. It's a bed and breakfast place now.' (SF.)

'THE CHORAL FESTIVAL of 1911. Well, well. I came to this in a four-in-hand brake from Taunton. Stopped at the Pipers Inn, on Walton Road, to change the horses and then off to the White Hart in Wells for stabling. And on to the Cathedral for the festival. All the choirs in the county were invited to take part. With tea in the Bishop's Barn afterwards. And a jolly good time was had by all!' (SF.)

'THEY'VE HAD PAGEANTS in Wells for donkey's years. Hundreds of years. This lot are got up as Romans for one that they had up at Stoberry Park in 1923. Roman helmets courtesy of the fire brigade by the look of it. Several hundred dressed up to show stages in the history of Wells.' (TT.)

'THESE TWO WERE GOT UP FOR A SHOW put on by one of the societies in Wells – pigeon fanciers or farmers' club or something – in 1910. I remember that there was no music during the day, 'cause they couldn't afford the licence, but then they had the Paulton Band playing for 'em in the evening.' (JS.)

Sporting Activity

'FATHER WAS THE CARETAKER of this Comrades' Club and one day I nipped home from school quickly to have a bit of practice on the billiard table, but Dick Loxton – the goalkeeper, here – was already in there playing. Asked me to nip out for some cigarettes. "All right, Dick." Bang! Father had come in behind me. Bang! "Mister Loxton to you." Bang! It was a lesson I never forgot.' (HL.)

'THE ATHLETIC CLUB used to organize lots of marathons and things like this. This is obviously an early one – could even be their first 'cause they only started up in 1886, or so I understand. Cost five bob to be a member.' (TT.)

'THIS WAS ANOTHER MARATHON – well, 20 miles or so, anyway. 'Twas to do with the November Carnival in 1908 and 18 of 'em ran from Bridgwater to Wells. Won by a chap called Mills from the Mendip Harriers in something under two and a half hours. A local chap – Allen – came in fifth.' (TT.)

'THESE MEN FROM THE QUOITS CLUB had their headquarters out on the Recreation Ground with a hut and a couple of clay beds. This was some time before I knew the place but, as kiddies, we used to go out and have a throw sometimes. I remember one big chap – David Kerr – whose quoits were too heavy for us to even lift, let alone throw. They used to compete against clubs from all around – Wookey, for example, and Radstock. That was always a good match, 'cause they had a number of England players in the Radstock team.' (GC.)

'ST CUTHBERT'S PAPER MILL ladies' football team in 1922. D'you know, I was on the Somerset list of referees and I refereed a team of Wells ladies once – not this one – against a team from Yeovil. Never again! Give me a men's team any day!' (GC.)

'THIS IS ST CUTHBERT'S BIBLE CLASS towards the end of the Great War. Very few of them left today. We had these Sports Days for two or three years but for one reason or another they petered out. That's the Reverend Lupton in the middle, alongside Alderman Wheeler.' (GC.)

'ON THE SAME DAY as the General Strike was called off they had this walking race to Glastonbury and back – arranged by two chaps called Mullins and Rolls who'd done the same thing themselves earlier in the year. Was won by "Brother" Dick Hippisley in two hours and four minutes. That's Dick with the knee-length shorts on. Everybody knew him – used to deliver newspapers all round the town. Very popular with all the people. I see Mr Wheeler's there again (with the white moustache). Supported everything, he did.' (TT.)

'I'M NOT ABSOLUTELY SURE ABOUT THIS ONE but I've always thought that these lads were the St Cuthbert's church team sometime in the 1890s. Smart looking bunch.' (JS.)

'THE WELLS ASYLUM ASSOCIATION FOOTBALL CLUB in 1908. They've always had sports clubs up there – football, tennis and so on. And the patients always used to get taken for walks in the countryside. But now they give them therapy to do. Not the same.' (NCo.)

'THE WELLS HARRIERS started up at Hinton Blewitt – still called Kennel Ground there now – then from there to Stanton Drew and from there to Wells. I used to love going out after them. Came out of school one day at 12 and they were just going off, so three or four of us went after them. Then we went to go back at 1.30 – proper time – and they were all coming out to go home. 'Twas 3.30 and time had gone so quickly we'd missed the whole of afternoon school. The teacher wrote a note to tell my father that I'd been absent and he read it and said, "I'd have done exactly the same!"' (AW.)

'GRANDFATHER always used to play for the Rugby Club in Wells more than 100 years ago. This is them just before the First World War. Their headquarters was always at the King's Head.' (HL.)

THE ST THOMAS STREET AREA of Wells was known as Turkey long before the country of Turkey came into being in 1923. On 3 May 1914 these lads from Turkey went on a bike ride to Weston-super-Mare. Just 13 weeks later some of them went on a much longer journey; one from which a number didn't return.

The First World War

MEN OF THE WELLS COMPANY in camp on Salisbury Plain with the 4th Battalion of the Somerset Light Infantry. At the outbreak of the war the Battalion was posted to India but without its Colonel – a GP called George Pollard from Midsomer Norton. To his dismay Col. Pollard was posted to Taunton as Chief Medical Officer.

'VOLUNTEERS FOR THE FRONT' in the Market Place in 1914. Within months of these pictures being taken would-be recruits, who had been rejected because of weak eyesight or similar defects, were being urged to re-apply. It was not long before standards were lowered again: 'Charles Adams appealed on the grounds that he had valvular disease of the heart. As a result of an accident he was incapacitated and awarded 10s. a week for life. Captain Mawer said he knew a doctor who had valvular disease of the heart who played golf and did a lot of things. Appeal dismissed.'

FIFTY FIVE DAYS after the start of the war, the Wells men of the Territorial 4th Battalion of the Somerset Light Infantry left the city to join other companies for their voyage to India aboard the *Braemar Castle*. Lieutenant Hicks and Sgt. Wheeler can be seen to the right of the flag. Beside the sergeant is his father, Alderman Wheeler. Despite promises from Lord Kitchener that these men would return to fight in Europe — as was their wish — the battalion remained in India for the duration of the war.

'THE 2ND BATTALION OF THE SOMERSET NATIONAL RESERVE were getting ready to go from the very beginning – this is some of them parading at the end of September in 1914. Another month and they'd gone. For my part I got my call-up on my 18th birthday and had to report to Taunton for my medical five days later. Before I knew it I was in the Devonshire Regiment.' (SF.)

'HERE ARE THE WELLS LOT of the Somerset Reserve leaving in October, 1914. Alderman Wheeler's there at the front again, see? Someone in the crowd here shouted to his mate to bring him back a parrot but he said he'd already got to bring back four elephants so he wouldn't have room.' (BD.)

260 COMPANY OF THE ARMY SERVICE CORPS. 'Everybody was charmed by the men who came here but there were hundreds and hundreds of them and they could be a damned nuisance. They had a right royal time too. Left dozens of kids behind when they left. That'll make 'em laugh, but 'tis true so why worry.' (IH.)

SOLDIERS FROM 133 COMPANY of the Army Service Corps, firing a salute at the funeral of Private George Smith in March, 1915. George had been an electrical engineer in Glasgow before the war but died of natural causes at the Cedars, in the Liberty – already, by that time, a military hospital.

JULY 1915 AND PRIVATE BOB FELTON, who was with this Ammunition Column on its afternoon off for a cricket match, writes home to his pals at an engineering works in Coventry: 'This beats work!'

LOCAL RESERVISTS pictured on the Athletic Ground during the war. At that time Wells men tended to enlist in regiments according to the district in which they lived – men from St Thomas', for example, favouring the Royal Horse Artillery. At the end of the second month of the war 650 of the 700 strong local North Somerset Yeomanry had confirmed their willingness to go to the Front. Within a month they had.

'I KNEW MOST OF THEM at the Hospital. Used to go up to play billiards and whist and things and they'd come to our place for a song at the old joanna. And then they'd come to our slaughterhouse – p'raps to learn a new job for after the war – but they soon ran off when the pigs began to squeal.' (IH.)

'BY THE TIME THIS WAS TAKEN Mr Wheeler was the Mayor and he did ever so much for the war. He was a wonderful man. Here he's taking charge of the farmers' sale to raise funds for the Red Cross at the cattle market. That's where the car park and bus station are now.' (BD.)

'EVERYONE TURNED OUT to see this motor transport company when they left Wells. This is where they were leaving the old cattle market where they used to park. My little brother, Tom, was standing with Mr Cottle, the painter, just to the left of where this was taken and later on I saw his picture in the shop window and went in and bought it. Tuppence.' (IH.)

'I WAS THERE WHEN THEY LEFT. Watched them drive all up through the High Street, here, and into Sadler Street, off on their way to France. There were transport sections in lots of villages round and about. Always seemed to be hundreds of soldiers about – and heaps of our own people had gone off elsewhere to do their bit. I wanted to go, too, but they wouldn't let me – reckoned I was too much use at home.' (IH.)

THERE ARE NO DATES to accompany these two pictures of patients at the Cedars Military Hospital but, for me, they epitomise the 'before and after' images of the men who fought in the First World War.

THIS YOUNG BLOOD still appears to have the swagger and confidence that many had when they left for the Front.

THIS OLD SOLDIER has seen it all (and would rather not have). Too often the same expressions and demeanour can be found on different photographs of the same man.

SOLDIERS, SAILORS AND CIVILIANS fill the Market Place for a Peace Day service in July 1919. However, the ranks of the Town Band have thinned considerably since 1914 and the company of ex-servicemen lining up behind them is no bigger than a single squad of recruits photographed on any day at the beginning of the war.

SECTION EIGHT

Calamities

'NO-ONE WHO WAS ALIVE THAT DAY would ever forget it. It was July 18th, 1926 and there had been a terrible storm in the night with thunder and lightning and hail – never known anything like it. Then, because we are down in a valley, the whole lot swept down from the Mendips and into Wells. It cascaded down, and there was nothing anyone could do about it.' (IH.)

'THE NATURAL COURSE for the water was down through Sadler Street and along the High Street and that's where it went. It sort of dammed off Chamberlain Street itself with all the boulders and muck but it played havoc elsewhere, going into shops and homes and filling cellars.' (IH.)

'WHEN IT WAS OVER, there was filth and muck all over the place – but you'd be surprised. People turned up from all over the place with buckets and shovels and brushes and set about cleaning it all up. Everyone mucked in and did what they could. They were very good. And why not? It was terrible.' (IH.)

'THE CURIOUS THING was that when visitors started turning up for their sight-seeing they had no idea that there'd been a storm 'cause it had been so localized. They only found out when their way was blocked by debris. It was a hell of a mess – and, 'course, no-one got any compensation.' (BD.)

'THIS MUST HAVE BEEN EARLIER than the 1926 storm going by their clothes. But what a storm it must have been to do that much damage. D'you know, there used to be some lovely trees round Wells, but so many have gone now. There is nothing more beautiful in the world than a nice wood of trees.' (IH.)

'I COLLECTED GLASS MARBLES from Scammell's ginger beer bottles 'til their factory got burnt down in 1914. And I had a cod bottle with a slit in it for collecting silver threepenny bits like you put in Christmas puddings. Gave it away when it got full. Go on – say I'm a fool, which I was in those days!' (IH.)

Societies of Wells

WORKMEN, CHURCHMEN AND BELL RINGERS pose beside St Cuthbert's new peal of bells just before it was hung in 1888.

IN THE MIDDLE OF THE SEVENTEENTH CENTURY Wells boasted 'fower and forty trayned Souldiers well armed, vizt. 23 Pykes, and 21 Musketts' ready to defend Somerset or England. When this photograph was taken, in 1878, The Wells (10th Somerset) Volunteer Rifle Corps was flourishing and had recently recruited 30 new members. Drill practice was held at 7 a.m. every Tuesday and Friday in the Market Place.

ON SUMMER EVENINGS during the Boer War, Lieutenant A.T. Powell led the 120 local members of K Company of the 3rd Battalion of Prince Albert's Somerset Light Infantry on route marches through the surrounding villages. Sometimes they would be accompanied by the Town Band, led by Mr Adlam, the local tobacconist, and more often than not they would stop off at some local hostelry for cider or ginger beer before returning to Wells.

'AT THIS TIME there were two bands in Wells. This was the one from the Brush Works but I was in the other one – the Town Band. Used to practice on Wednesdays and Saturdays up on the Recreation Ground. No bandstand – used to have great big beer barrels with planks laid over them. Then, when we'd finished for the day, we'd have to take it all down again.' (G.C.)

'THE MAYOR AND CORPORATION. That's well before my time — that's before 1890, when John Holloway was the Mayor and the big bald Alderman is Mr Everett. The mace carriers have got the same outfits and maces as when I was the senior mace bearer. Queen Elizabeth I granted a Charter that said that Wells could have a Mayor, seven Masters and sixteen Councillors — so some of them must have been away on holiday when this was taken!' (SF.)

'IT WAS A GREAT MISTAKE when they closed down the Theological College in Wells. They used to come here after they'd been to university to be trained as vicars – that was the general theme of it. More than one of them who trained here came back later to be the Bishop.' (TT.)

'THAT'S ONE OF THE MANY CLUBS IN WELLS at the turn of the century. They had Druids, Shepherds, Foresters, Buffaloes, Templars and two or three others besides. These are the Oddfellows. My father belonged to the Oddfellows – he was a wheelwright by profession. Before these came along every village had its own club, with club days and suppers and special staves with brass tops on – friendly societies which took care of their members' well-being – but this sort of organisation put an end to those clubs.' (SF.)

'THE ST JOHN'S AMBULANCE MEN, in about 1928 or 30 I'd say. I reckon that's Dr Mullins in the plain clothes. He was a surgeon doctor in the navy and then did a lot to get cricket going in Wells after the First War. He lived up on the junction of the Bath Road and the Bristol Road. Had a collection of old armour and weapons and when the Home Guard was formed in the last war they borrowed his old pikes and things to parade with, would you believe!' (HL.)

Wells – A Country Town

'THE CATHEDRAL taken by someone up on Milton Hill. This was sometime round the turn of the century, I'd say. You can see Dulcote over there on the right. That was so beautiful once, but now its nearly all quarried away. Dreadful.' (IH.)

'GRANDFATHER WAS A FARM LABOURER and sometimes I used to come into Wells with him on his cart. Him and Grandmother brought up 11 children in their cottage on the hill, with about an acre of ground. Half of that was pasture, where he used to keep the old pony, and about quarter was orchard with the rest garden. Couple of pigstys and 24 or 30 hens. And that man and his wife were happier than anyone of my generation have been.' (HL.)

THE SOMERSET AGRICULTURAL SHOW was held on the Bishop's Park in 1906 – as it had been ten years earlier. Agricultural machinery exhibits, like the vertical steam engine and Blackstone's cornmills seen here, were among the increasing number of mechanical implements being exhibited at such fairs but, on this occasion, there were still all the traditional features in evidence with 172 contestants in the horse show, to say nothing of the 65 ladies butter-making and the eight smiths a'smithying.

CONTESTANTS in the Wells ploughing competition of 1920. 'These fellows used to get together for ploughing matches, hedging matches, thatching, all sorts of things like that. And jolly skillful they were, too. Ran classes in 'em an' all.' (TT.)

'THE SOMERSET AGRICULTURAL SHOW in 1907. That's where I first saw English pottery made. My two sisters and me had pretty little vases each with oak leaves and flowers. And I saw butter and cheese made and cows and pigs, poultry, rabbits and bantams. I wanted a bantam but Dad said no.' (IH.)

A VIEW FROM THE CATHEDRAL. looking towards the Mendips in the 1890s. Stoberry Park can be seen in the upper left of the picture. 'That's all built up so much now, isn't it. Did you know that Queen Mary lived in one of those houses at the bottom for some time during the war?' (IH.)

'WHERE'S THIS THEN? Cheddar one way and Glastonbury the other. Ah, that's down the bottom of the Portway. That looks like a Mr Griffin with the dear old pony – but I don't know for sure.' (IH.)

'NOBODY SEEMS IN ANY GREAT HURRY, do they? Reckon it must be lunch time with those workmen taking a break outside the Bishop's Barn and the kiddies out from school on the swings. What would you say, the 1880s or '90s?' (BD.)

'THERE WERE OVER 900 PATIENTS at the Mendip Hospital when I went up there to look for work in 1932. It was a damn good place to work – and, come to that, not a bad place to be a patient in, either.' (SF.)

THE MAGNIFICENT VIEW OF WELLS from Tor Woods. The Reverend John Skinner of Camerton was a frequent visitor to the city where he delighted in the beauty of its architecture. On one visit, in 1817, he 'made some sketches of the figures outside the Cathedral. Afterwards I was introduced to a curious character residing in the city, usually denominated Conjuror Paine. He had, I find, a hand at everything, electricity, magic, turning, carpentry, collecting fossils, gardening, doctoring and moreover he is a book collector. I purchased one off him, denominated the "Silver Bell", written about 150 years ago, and a fossil for which I paid him six times its value.'

SECTION ELEVEN

Children

THE QUEEN OF THE MAY — a prize-winning float in the November Carnival of 1906. 'Great competition there was to be the May Queen in Wells but this picture must have been taken in the morning 'cause that afternoon there was a cloudburst and the whole affair was a washout. I was eight.' (IH.)

'THE BOYS AND TEACHERS with Revd Beresford – Johnny Longbottom – up at St Thomas School. 'Bout 1895. I hated school. Never liked it – but that was my fault, not the school's. The teachers were ever so good but I had no time for homework. Had to go home to look after the poultry. "You go to school to learn, not to bring homework home here." Things were very different.' (IH.)

'THIS IS REVD BERESFORD AGAIN, up at the Deanery. I imagine that those must be choristers with him, but I don't recognise them – must be back in the 1890s at least. But that's Mr Beresford, all right – we often used to see him going off on horseback to visit the villages round and about. A good man – took a lot of interest in children.' (IH.)

'THESE ARE THE BOYS at the Central School in 1905 or 6 when Mr Knight was the headmaster. His daughter there, on the right, married a Mr Brook who started up Oakleigh School, the little private concern. Mrs Knight, sitting in the middle with the cane, looks to be more the boss than her husband!' (NC.)

ON WEDNESDAY, 17 AUGUST, 1910, the Reverend and Mrs E. Jubb threw open the grounds of their home, Tower House, for a Grand Al Fresco Concert that was organised by St Thomas' Parish Council. This dumbell display given by the Church Lads' Brigade was one of numerous attractions.

'NOW I RECKON that that's about 1908 or 9 'cause my brother's on there. They're all from the Central School but I can't work out what they're doing. P'raps they're off on some kind of outing or maybe there for Mr Phillips to take pictures of them. There was nothing he didn't take!' (IH.)

'AH, THE DICK WHITTINGTON PANTOMIME at St Thomas School during the First War. That's me – Jack, the cook's son, looking between Dick and the king. Florrie Lockyear was the cook and May Allen was Dick. Fancied myself no end in my rigout.' (NC.)

'THAT'S MY CLASS at St Thomas School in 1914 with Gwennie Woodburn, the pupil teacher. That's me in the middle row with the pinafore – like my sister's wearing in the back row. The schoolmaster's house is at the back. There were great dividing doors between us and the boys' part.' (NC.)

'I'M TOLD THESE NIPPERS had been fishing for tiddlers in the moat at the Bishop's Palace before the last war. I used to go up there often before the first one – used to save cigarette cards and one day I was leaning over the drawbridge watching the fish and a whole lot of them fell out of my pocket into the water there. "The Fishing Bait" set they were, and I lost the lot. Had the complete set but for number 19.' (IH.)

'THERE WERE HUNDREDS AND HUNDREDS OF GIRL GUIDES in Wells that day. It was on a Saturday in 1926 and they were here for a county rally. First they had a service at the Cathedral and then they marched all round the town and back here again for dancing and things on the Green.' (TT.)

'THIS IS ANOTHER LOT OF GIRL GUIDES but this is from another meeting several years later. They've had their rally and done their sight-seeing and now they're having a bit of a snack and a rest by the moat. Don't blame 'em either!' (TT.)

Commerce

'THERE'S MR BARNES in the door of his double-fronted shop where you could buy everything from a pin to a steamroller. That's Woolworths now. Used to have annual bike sales – had Triumphs, Hudsons, Quadrants, Sunbeams, Enfields, Humbers – the lot.' (FG.)

'OH, WAYS WAS THE BEST. Very high class. It had a lovely trade and when I first started – before they got that van – all the deliveries were by horse and cart. Mr Beer, the manager, is on here, and so are Mr Pullen and Mr Tripp and Mr Angell. That's me by the post – the other girl was from Belgium. A lot of the delivering was done by that little lad with his handcart – told me not so long ago that the boss bought him a pint of milk every day he was there!' (NC.)

THIS SUPERB SELECTION OF BISCUITS was displayed in the window of Ways, in the High Street. Eminent biscuit historians tell me that it must have been photographed in 1901.

'BERT PHILLIPS'S SHOP was a very important one 'cause if he hadn't been here you wouldn't have had half the pictures for this book of yours! He was a dapper little man – ever-so businesslike.' (BD.)

'USED TO TAKE MOTHER'S MACHINE DOWN HERE to the Singer sewing machine shop in St Cuthbert's Street. Don't remember the name of the people who ran it though – think they may have been Singer's own people.' (IH.)

'WHEN THESE PEOPLE FIRST CAME to Broad Street you could only buy tea from them – all sorts of tea, but only tea. After that they began to sell everything in the grocery line. It was a good shop, ever so clean inside, and nice smelling, but very small. On the left of it was Mr Styles, who made and sold furniture, and on the other side was Mr Nelson's foreign meat shop.' (IH.)

'THERE HAVE BEEN FAIRS here in Wells for more than 850 years – this one was in 1897. The proper drapery shop on the !eft there was owned by Charlie Tucker in those days, but we knew it as Mrs Tucker's – had to go up two ever-so-steep steps to get in; too steep for me – Mother had to haul me up them. Next to it was the old ironmongery – Tinny Reakes's – a tinsmith, also a member of the council and one-time mayor.' (IH.)

'SAME MARKET. SAME DAY. Notice the little group of gipsy caravans at the back? I remember these things coming in but they put a stop to it but I don't know fer why. It may have been 'cause they liked to park their horses on other people's property. Never bothered to ask, mind.' (IH.)

'OH, I KNOW THIS ONE — on the corner of Mill Street and the High Street. Always very, very dark inside and run by tubby old Mr Tyte, with a huge long apron and tiny little glasses right on the end of his nose. Would always rub his hands — "And what can I do for you. Sir?" Always.' (HL.)

'MR ADLAM'S TOBACCO SHOP and Mrs Vincent's butchery at the end of the High Street. Always two sorts of butchers up to the Great War. Ours was like this, for pork and poultry (and cheese and eggs and the like — butter fourpence–sixpence a pound). The others were for beef and mutton.' (IH.)

AN IGNOMINIOUS TASK for these two oxen whose job it was to promote the Bovo Gravy Powder made by Ebeneezer Roberts and Sons of London. One wonders how many trips these beasts made before they themselves became the subject of the advertising.

CLARE'S STORE in the Market Place in 1912. Their delivery van, on the left, was built by the Chewton Mendip Motor Works and Mr Clare was so pleased with it that he wrote to the firm: 'When you delivered it last August, we immediately put it upon the Army Supply Work, in the worst of weather, upon some of the most difficult roads in Somersetshire, without a single breakdown, our drivers having only had one month's tuition at your works. Since that time the van has been on the road daily and with the exception of the front tyres (these are pneumatic) we have had no expense whatever, other than Petrol and Oil.'

'ONCE UPON A TIME there were permanent market stalls all along the middle of the High Street – called Middle Row. The stalls were known as Shambles, like they've got in Shepton and elsewhere. Shambles were really reckoned to be for butchers but all sorts of traders used them. And built up over the top of them was a big public hall where they used to sell linen. That all went about 250 years ago.' (TT.)

'SADLER STREET. Just where that delivery van is parked on the right was Mr Ricketts' chemist shop. Then there was a harness shop and then the sweet shop. Real sweets, mind you. Humbugs, liquorice, boiled sweets, shrimps – nothing but sweets. Cheap and dear. When Dad used to go to the chemist this little tot was left sitting in the cart and the lady from the sweet shop would always come out and give me something. "It's all right my dear, I know your daddy." She gave me a brass shoe horn once. Still got it.' (IH.)

'THIS IS ON THE CORNER OF QUEEN STREET and St Cuthbert Street and was taken before the First World War. Mr Wyatt used to be here on the right – making harnesses and things for horses and then there was Creases, the grocers – good grocers. And over on the left used to be the Queen's Head pub what Mr Wilton – the Town Cryer – had made into the shop there, selling baskets and furniture and toys and buckets and things. All sorts. Hey! Look at those men on the roof!' (IH.)

'ON THE RIGHT – where those carts are parked – was Somerset House, just one of any number of pubs in the High Street. There used to be The Black Boy, The Queen's Arms, The Catherine Wheel, The Angel, The Hare and Hounds and more – not to mention the ones that are still there! And did you know that the City Arms cellar used to be the town gaol, and where they stored the gallows and stocks and ducking stool?' (TT.)

'BEHIND THOSE MEN ON THE RIGHT was a most wonderful corn and seed shop – another dark shop run by an old boy – tall with a little velvet cap, something like the Jewish people wear, and a long apron. Very few shop fittings then and all along the left were lovely new hessian sacks open with different things in – wheat, maize and so on – and in each sack was a lovely polished mahogany wooden shovel. And all up the other side was a mass of drawers – a mass of them – and every one had different little seeds in them. I shall always remember that shop.' (HL.)

'1905. THE YEAR WE CAME TO LIVE IN WELLS from Coxley. Some of these shops were beautiful places, and some of them were little gold mines then. We had ours in Queen Street and used to do a lot of trading with people who came into Wells for their shopping. Folk 'ould come in and place their orders for meat and then go off to do other things. It was a lovely time.' (IH.)

Transport

'WHAT A GLORIOUS PICTURE — must be round the turn of the century. And that's how they used to travel when I was a young 'un. Looks here like we've got a bunch of the lads off from the White Hart to a footer match or summat. Glorious!' (TT.)

CHARLIE JEWELL (second from the left) with his fleet of vehicles at his garage in Priory Road during the First World War (the little girls were presumably there to swell the ranks!). 'There used to be a fried fish shop there before the garage, but it caught fire. The man caught his apron alight while he was frying the fish and up it all went. The Fire Brigade didn't have enough water to put it out so they had to go to the river behind. Remember it well.' (IH.)

'THAT COULD BE FRANK CARDWELL at the steering wheel of Mr Jewell's Napier. It's certainly not him at the back 'cause Frank'd never take a back seat in anything! One thing he got up to was to sit on the handlebars of a bike and ride it backwards all the way up Broad Street. Nice man.' (IH.)

'CHARLIE HOWARD, driving the Bishop's old Crossley in the Market Place. 'Bout 1932ish, I'd say. Lived in a nice house down in South Street. Charlie, that is, not the Bishop.' (SF.)

'NOW, THIS HAS TO BE THE MAYOR'S CARRIAGE. Pretty smart, isn't it. Always bags of pomp and ceremony attached to this sort of thing, there was. One of the people who looked after these coaches was Mr Coles, who kept The King's Head. People with that job were known as Jobmasters. He used to have a plate up outside his place with that engraved on it.' (TT.)

'THE POSTMASTER'S BRAKE outside the old post office in the Market Place. See how it's all open behind? That was filled in the way it is now about 1903. They used to use this thing to fetch mail from the station and take letters out to Shepton Mallet and all over the place, didn't they? The letters were in bags made by people in prison. Ever so well made. We had some and used them as door mats. Don't know how we came by them though. That's very old, I reckon. At least 100 years.' (IH.)

'THIS IS ANOTHER PLACE where I delivered parcels of eggs and meat and stuff – bacon, fourpence a pound – the ostlers' yard at the back of the White Hart. I knew everybody's cart and just put the parcels in the right ones. Got a penny for it sometimes.' (IH.)

Wells at Work

'THIS YOUNGSTER has come down into Wells from the Mendip Hospital to get parcels of some sort. You can just make out 'Somerset & Bath Asylum – Wells' on the side of his cart. As far as foodstuffs were concerned they were pretty well self-supporting. Had their own bakery and butchery and farm and grew all their own vegetables and fruit. Always a highly efficient place.' (SF.)

WORKERS AT THE WELLS BRUSH FACTORY in the early 1940s, where a wide range of brooms, besoms and scourers were once hand-made for world-wide export. Their products included Turk's head churn brushes, bottle brushes, bass brooms, deck scrubs, soft brushes, sweeping brushes and a cupboard-full of other creations. It seems that the success of their products depended largely upon local timber, South American mule hair, thrump-hemp, hot pitch and 'a special twist of the wrist' at the gluing stage.

ROAD MENDING IN WELLS in the early 1920s with an Aveling and Porter road-roller and a horse-drawn tar cart. 'They both belonged to Neville Grenville who lived at The Court at Butleigh. These things were his – they actually belonged to him – and he hired them out for use all over Somerset. And he was very influential in the cider business of the county. He was an interesting man.' (IH.)

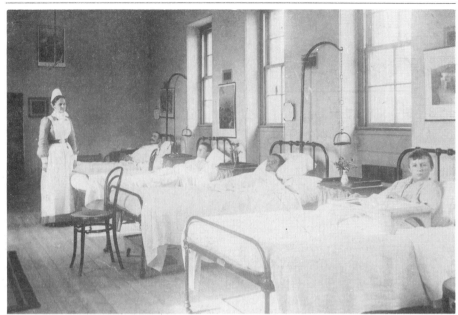

'THE COTTAGE HOSPITAL (above) was all there was in those days – two wards, one for men and one for women. Always had a good name. The Priory Hospital (below) was The Union then, you know, the workhouse. The tramps – the milestone inspectors – the men who walked the roads to keep their independence, used to go over the stile into the field behind to hide their pennies in the stone walls so's not to have to pay for their overnight stay. They used to dig some garden or chop bundles of logs instead. I used to enjoy talking to them. I liked them.' (IH.)

'MR TINKNELL had that place. Our pony, Tommy, could very well be in there when this was taken. When I was ten years old I used to drive him all over the place and think nothing of it. Used to come up here for him to be shod. Tommy never minded and while he was being done I used to go in and have a bit of a chat with the cook. Still got one of Tommy's shoes in the cupboard now.' (IH.)

STEEPLEJACKS from William Bray's building firm working on the South Transept of the Cathedral in 1905. 'Just look at them – no scaffolding, just ladders and planks and ropes. I ran away when I saw them 'cause I was afraid one of them would fall on me. Mr Bray was who Grandfather worked for – for fifteen shillings a week.' (IH.)

'BLIMEY! Look at all the policemen – here for the Assizes I shouldn't doubt. Not all from Wells, that's for sure. About 1895ish, I'd say. Mr Tait's there in the middle with his bowler and he's in the right place too, 'cause his word was law. Kept the wine bar above The Star. He was one of the nobility of Wells – had something to do with everything. Always well respected though.' (IH.)

'THEY'RE SELLIN' THINGS, LOOK. He's got a roll of oilcloth and cane chairs — all second-hand stuff. They're travellers. Poor folk, but not gypsies. Might well have been members of the Bower family who used to camp out on Butleigh Down before World War One.' (IH.)

Streetscapes

THE WESLEYAN CHAPEL in Southover in 1903. Seventeen years earlier – according to the *Somerset Advertiser* – they had an 'entertainment consisting of songs, trios, recitations in the school rooms. The Revd W.L. Beadon being unable to attend there was a very appreciative audience'.

THE CATHEDRAL seen from St Thomas Street in the mid-1930s. The Goat Inn can be seen just beyond the telegraph pole and, at the bottom of the road, is Alderman Sealey's garage.

'BROAD STREET got its name 'cause it's so wide and it's wide because there used to be more buildings running down the middle of it. Used to be called Wet Lane and Watery Lane, too. See the India and China Tea shop on the left? And Mr Adlam's and Mrs Vincent's [120] at the top?' (TT.)

'SADLER STREET – that was named after an MP that Wells had a few hundred years ago. There's Rumming's shop and the tobacco store next to the White Hart, and Wicks's – high class shop for curtains and things. And then there was a bun shop – caterers, you know.' (IH.)

'SEE THE SWAN OVER THE ARCHWAYS at the Swan Hotel? They reckon that that was already a very old place when 'twas rebuilt about 500 years ago. There was s'posed to be another door up the wall on the left of the swan so folk could get straight from the tops of stagecoaches into the hotel.' (TT.)

'FIFTEEN YEARS BEFORE he started the State of Pennsylvania in America, William Penn – who was a Quaker – came to Wells and preached several times to thousands of people from the windows of the Crown Hotel there, just on the right of the conduit. Got arrested for it the first time.' (FG.)

'THAT CANON was put in the Market Place after the Crimean war – in the last war they had a field gun parked there. Up until 1779 there used to be a Guildhall and market hall built where those farmers are standing and those and other buildings took up most of the space between the conduit and the Bishop's Eye. It was in the Guildhall that Judge Jeffries – the Hanging Judge – ordered 99 men to be hung at the Bloody Assize after the Monmouth Rebellion in 1685.' (FG.)

THE ORIGINAL CONDUIT in the Market Place was put there by Bishop Beckington in 1451. He had the water piped from the Palace grounds to this point after which it ran down the sides of the High Street – or Great Street as it was known in those days – cleaning the muck from the street and what the tradesmen had thrown out as it went. This conduit, here, was built later, in 1799, at a cost of £150, 'cause the first one had begun to tumble down.' (FG.)

Hostelries

'THERE'S THE MITRE'S BUS bringing customers up from the station. They all had their own buses like that in those days – The Mitre, The Star, The Swan – all the same. Frank Cardwell drove for The Swan and Gilbert Coles drove for The King's Head. We used to collect the stuff from the horses for the gardens, but not if it came from Gilbert Coles's horses 'cause he never fed them enough for it to be any good!' (HL.)

'WE USED TO COME UP HERE to the Mitre for dances in the First War. Thruppence a time. This is looking out through from the back into Sadler Street. Just on the left of where that man is standing by himself they've got all the timetables for the Great Western Railway posted up.' (IH.)

'THAT'S VERY OLD, THE MERMAID. Used to have some right rumpuses down there – specially on May Day when the gypsies used to come in with their ponies and horses to sell. All running up and down the road outside to show them off. Squabbles and fighting and the police coming to sort it out. Harry Stark, the old chap who had the place, was once asked if he kept the Mermaid and he said, "Not damned likely. The Mermaid keeps me."' (SF.)

'THE WHITE HART was always a good place. Mr Dawe used to serve good food there too, and coffee, as well as beer and stuff. Doesn't look as if he let children or dogs in though, does it?' (IH.)

'OAKHILL BREWERY – established 1767. Looks like their drayman got more than he bargained for when he let them take a photograph of him here. Collected quite a crowd, didn't he. That's delivering at The Globe in 1908.' (TT.)

AN ELEVATED VIEW of St Thomas Street in the 1890s. It is just possible to make out two covered wagons, one of which is on its way into Wells and the other making a delivery at The New Inn. 'There were lots of pubs up there – The Goat, The Lamb and The Fountain and another one I forget. Quite often they were used by the miners from Radstock way, specially if there was a carnival or the like in Wells next day. Used to have a wild old time up there. So wild that the places had to shut down sometimes!' (IH.)

'IS THAT WHAT IT LOOKS LIKE INSIDE THE GLOBE? Must pop in there sometime! Do you know, there used to be three or four pubs in every street in Wells – more than 50 at the turn of the century I've been told – but it was never really a boozy place. We're very central, you see, and the farmers and the miners and the quarrymen all used to come in here for a drink from time to time. Apart from the ones we've talked about there was The Boot, The Three Pigeons, The Forester's Arms, The Royal Oak, The Three Cups, The White Bull, The Bull's Head and heaps more besides. But it wasn't a boozy place. Honestly.' (IH.)

The Second World War

'THERE WERE HEAPS of these salvage drives during the Second World War. It took about 40 tons of salvage to raise £100. Looks like one of Mr Jewell's lorries they've filled up. My war effort was looking after 200 fowls. I remember one Christmas when we were too tired to eat our dinner. War, war, war. I hate it.' (IH.)

'DURING THE WEAPONS WEEK in March 1942, they were out to raise something like £65,000 to adopt HMS *Fleetwood*. You can see the sort of turnout that there was. One thousand soldiers were on parade that day. And they raised the money – goodness knows how.' (TT.)

'WE WERE ALWAYS HAVING FUND-RAISING EFFORTS – to buy Spitfires and things. The Mayor was a Mr Kippax – sort of chap if you knocked him down with a mallet he'd bounce right back up. We had a great thermometer thing in the Market Place to show how much we collected. And it was a hell of a lot.' (HL.)

'A FEW DAYS AFTER THE WAR ENDED we had this parade through the town with Alderman Sealey taking the salute in the Market Place. I remember that there were soldiers and scouts and guides and ATS and Red Cross people all there. This is the ATS girls waiting their turn to take part.' (TT.)

'THERE WERE TERRIFIC PARTIES when it was over. Cars and bikes and shops and houses were all covered in red, white and blue. Pubs sold out. Children saw fireworks for the first time in their lives. There was dancing in the streets – someone led a conga through a septic tank but no-one seemed to care. Heal's funfair was in Wells at the time and did terrific business. Everyone went barmy.' (TT.)

FINALLY, Wells celebrated in the way that it knows best, with a Thanksgiving Carnival. After this, things slowly began to get back to something like normal. One of the things that happened was that the camp for German prisoners of war in Stoberry Park was disbanded. And then my dad came home.

ACKNOWLEDGEMENTS

I have been preparing this book, on and off, for about six years but only when I met Jeffrey Allen, who lives in Wells, did the whole thing really gain any momentum. He was halfway up a ladder when I first met him and by the time he had reached the bottom rung he had offered me the full use of his impressive collection of photographs. Jeff, probably more than anyone else, enabled me to finish the book. The other main source of photographs was the magnificent collection held by Wells Museum and I am indebted to the present and past two Curators and their Management Committees, without whose generosity and co-operation the book would be markedly the poorer. The vast majority of their photographs were taken by the Phillips family, who created a unique photographic history of the city. It is a collection of major importance and I was fortunate indeed to have access to it.

Others who kindly lent me pictures include Mrs Bishop, Peter Carter, Grenville and Nellie Chappell, *Country Life*, Bert Dando, Dick Graham, Elsie Hillier, Lis Howell, Richard Maggs, Roger Noble, David Patch, Catherine Pollard, Arthur Rice, John Sidney, Mr and Mrs Stock, Bob Weare and Kathleen Willcox.

Wherever possible I have used the words of the people of Wells as captions for the pictures and these came from Mr and Mrs Chapel (GC. + NC.), Nellie Corp (NCo.), Bert Dando (BD.), Stan Fudge (SF.), the avuncular Fred Gibbons (FG.), who was surely born to be the city's Town Crier, Ivy Herniman (IH.), Edward Hutton, Harold Lane (HL.), Tom Randall – who allowed me to use material from his own forthcoming book on the Mendip Motor Company of Chewton Mendip, Arthur Rice (AR.), John Sidney (JS.) and Tommy Tucker (TT.).

I am grateful, too, to the Rt Revd George Carey, Bishop of Bath and Wells for graciously agreeing to write the foreword to the book and to those whose names follow for their directions, suggestions and reading: Bob Bates, Jean Imray, Roger Noble, De Pickford, Margaret Rice, D.C. Tudway, Barbara Ward, *The Wells Journal* – for allowing me such easy access to their archives, Doris White and Austin and Ethel Wookey – who help me just by being there.

Finally, once again I thank my family, Birgitta, John and Lis, for putting up with me.

CJH